# Borderline Personality
# Disorder Journal

# Borderline Personality Disorder *Journal*

## DBT Prompts and Practices to Manage Symptoms and Achieve Balance

**Whitney Frost**, LPC, C-DBT

ROCKRIDGE
PRESS

Interior and Cover Designer: Mando Daniel
Art Producer: Melissa Malinowsky
Editor: Brian Sweeting
Production Editor: Matthew Burnett
Production Manager: Jose Olivera

iStock, cover; all other illustrations used under license from Shutterstock.
Author photo courtesy of Amber Braxton, Valuable Gem Photography.

Paperback ISBN: 978-1-63878-491-3
R0

For those who have the courage to keep fighting every day, don't give up.
Your fight is not over.

# Contents

# Introduction

My name is Whitney Frost, and I am a Licensed Professional Counselor and a Certified DBT Therapist. I began my work with DBT borderline personality disorder (BPD) in 2016, when I was trained by Behavioral Tech, a Linehan Institute training company. I continued my professional practice in a DBT intensive program at the Jefferson Center in Lakewood, Colorado. I am passionate about helping women with borderline personality disorder find symptom relief and freedom from the stigma that often accompanies diagnosis.

While the struggles associated with BPD are often unfairly stigmatized, having a diagnosis—or a suspected diagnosis—of BPD is not the end of the world. Borderline personality disorder can be overcome and controlled through some essential skills and symptom management.

Dialectical behavior therapy (DBT) is currently considered the gold standard treatment for those struggling with borderline personality disorder. Keep in mind that you do not have to have a diagnosis of BPD to benefit from DBT skills. Those who struggle with impulsivity, emotional dysregulation, emotional distress intolerance, or interpersonal relational difficulties can benefit from DBT skills. This journal will guide you toward better managing some of the symptoms and struggles associated with BPD in a nonjudgmental, self-paced way.

# How to Use This Journal

Throughout this journal, you will notice a variety of prompts, exercises, and affirmations based on the skills you are working on in the section. Each section has a different focus for managing a different type of symptom of borderline personality disorder. In order to gain the most benefit from these exercises, it is recommended that you work through this journal in order, from beginning to end. But this is, of course, your journal, and you can use it however you think is most beneficial. This journal can be used alone or as a companion to the *Borderline Personality Disorder Workbook* (Rockridge Press, 2021) if you are looking for more resources for managing your symptoms.

> *This journal is not intended to be a diagnostic tool, nor is it meant to replace or substitute for mental health counseling or psychiatric services. If you are experiencing thoughts of suicide, self-harm, or thoughts of harming others, please reach out to the National Suicide Prevention Hotline at 1-800-273-8255 or go to your nearest emergency room.*

## Unpacking Borderline Personality Disorder

From the DBT standpoint, BPD is not a hereditary or genetic behavioral health condition. It is believed that BPD is created by various factors within one's environment, including being biologically sensitive to emotional stimuli, having intense emotions, having a harder time resisting impulses, being in an environment that invalidates your emotions or tells you that your emotions are wrong, and being in an environment that reinforces the emotions and actions that cause the most trouble. This theory is referred to as the biosocial theory of BPD.

BPD can present differently for everyone based on their biology, social situation, chemical composition, and medical history. There are no medications specifically intended to treat or cure BPD, but medication might be used to treat certain subsets of symptoms that come along with BPD, like depression and anxiety. However, DBT is considered the best treatment modality for BPD as it is evidence-based, meaning it has been proven by ample research to be effective at managing various symptoms of BPD. This journal will walk you through the core principles and skills of DBT and give you journal prompts, exercises, and affirmations to put these skills to use in your own life.

# A Brief Introduction to Dialectical Behavior Therapy

Marsha Linehan, a clinical psychologist at the University of Washington and a Zen master, is the creator of dialectical behavior therapy. Dr. Linehan is a professor and researcher who has provided major contributions to the behavioral health community, including evidence-based treatments for highly suicidal and severely mentally ill communities. DBT was built on the principles of cognitive behavioral therapy (CBT) with a focus on managing chronically suicidal patients with a diagnosis of BPD.

DBT uses four types of treatment: individual therapy, group skills training, phone coaching, and a therapist consultation team meeting. Using these modalities, the goal of DBT is to help one both accept and change unhealthy or destructive patterns in thinking, feeling, and behavior. In DBT, learning to simultaneously accept and change is referred to as a "dialectic," or the act of acknowledging two opposites to be equally true at the same time. For example, it can be sunny *and* raining, or you can be happy for a friend who got into college *and* be sad they are leaving. Dialectics and this way of thinking is seen throughout the DBT skills and therapy orientation as a way of challenging the "black and white thinking" patterns exhibited by many people with BPD.

In addition to the four types of treatment, DBT is built upon four core principles, or modules: Mindfulness, Distress Tolerance, Emotion Regulation, and Interpersonal Effectiveness. These skills will be explained throughout this journal for your exploration and better understanding.

## Core Principle 1: Mindfulness

Mindfulness is the heart and soul of DBT. Its skills are sprinkled throughout all DBT skills. Mindfulness is rooted in the idea of connecting your quality of awareness of everyday living and your quality of presence in everyday life. Mindfulness is finding the balance between doing and being within your life, and living with your eyes wide open. In future sections, we will discuss how to implement and use the "what" and "how" skills of mindfulness practice: *observe, describe, participate, nonjudgmentally, one-mindfully*, and *effectively*. The idea of using mindfulness to manage BPD is rooted in the idea of being present in the current moment to gain a better understanding of how you feel, as well as being aware of your surroundings to better manage and reduce distress and implement skills effectively.

## Core Principle 2: Distress Tolerance

Distress tolerance skills are meant to manage a perceived crisis without making it worse, along with helping us accept our reality when we cannot change it. This set of skills is meant to help you survive what might feel like a crisis without resorting to your old patterns of BPD behavior and making the crisis worse. A crisis may be something associated with impulsivity or interpersonal struggles, such as a conflict with a friend or a partner, overdrawing your bank account, or getting a speeding ticket. Distress tolerance skills help you survive a situation when you cannot immediately change the outcome or sort out your feelings, allowing you to make a decision that will meet your goals. The goal is finding peace with yourself and being content with your circumstances. This is accomplished with help from radical acceptance, a skill that will be taught later in this journal.

## Core Principle 3: Emotion Regulation

For many individuals with BPD, regulating painful emotions is a common problem they seek help with, given their tendency toward high emotional sensitivity. Emotion regulation skills aid in naming emotions, understanding emotions, changing unwanted emotions, and understanding what emotions do for you. These skills take practice in order for you to feel competent using them, and they can be difficult to grasp if you have a history of invalidation of strong emotional responses throughout your life from others who did not understand. Emotions are not simple, singular events. They occur with a primary emotion followed by secondary emotional responses, such as anger that is followed by sadness. By using emotion regulation skills, you will learn how to name, manage, and change both your primary and secondary emotions and your responses to them to feel more effective and in control.

## Core Principle 4: Interpersonal Effectiveness

When navigating life with BPD, relationships can be a challenge. Between splitting (having a hard time seeing both the good and bad in people or situations), abandonment concerns, and flipping between idealization and devaluation of those closest to you, it can be difficult to manage positive and negative relationships. Interpersonal relationship skills help you manage conflicts within relationships, effectively end and maintain relationships, ask for what you need without manipulation, validate yourself, meet new friends, and find self-respect. Often, we lose our sense of self within relationships by meeting others' needs and goals while forgetting about our own. Interpersonal relationship skills allow us to find the "middle path" in meeting our goals without damaging the relationship.

*I am grounded; I am capable and in control of my actions and emotions.*

# PART ONE

# Mindfulness: Take Notice Before You Take Action

In this section, we will explore prompts and exercises centered on mindfulness, and how these skills can help reduce and manage symptoms associated with BPD. We will expand on the mindfulness "what" and "how" skills in this section, as well as practice various ways to bring mindfulness into your life. Feel free to refer back to "Core Principle 1: Mindfulness" on page xi for a refresher on what mindfulness is as you work through these prompts and exercises.

# Basics of Mindfulness

Mindfulness is the practice of living with intention and aware-ness of your present moment, turning off "autopilot" and being an active participant in your life. Mindfulness comes without judgment, which means not evaluating, avoiding, or blocking the unpleasant. Let go of attachment and accept things as they come to you without holding onto the past or anticipating the future. This can be practiced anywhere, anytime, and while doing anything. Mindfulness is especially helpful when dealing with the symptoms of BPD, as it allows us to be fully present and aware of all the components of a situation before acting impulsively or from an emotional mindset.

How are you currently practicing mindfulness? What areas of your life would improve if you were more present and mind-ful? How do you see yourself incorporating mindfulness into your life? Where in your day do you think being mindful would be most effective?

_____

_____

_____

_____

_____

_____

_____

# Mindfulness in Practice

While you think about incorporating mindfulness into your daily life, explore how it will be most helpful in each area of your life and how it can improve these areas (e.g., communication, relationships, timeliness):

Intimate Relationships:

_____

_____

_____

Work:

_____

_____

_____

Family:

_____

_____

_____

Friendships:

_____

_____

_____

Personal/Self-Improvement:

_____

_____

_____

_____

_____

_____

_____

_____

_____

_____

_____

# Bubbles of Mindfulness

Find a sink and soap. Fill the sink with warm water and soap, then submerge your hands. For the next minute, notice how the bubbles look: their individual sizes, colors, and shapes. Notice the smell of the soap. Try observing your hands in the soapy water without judgment. Notice how the water feels on your hands, how it moves, and how it looks as you move your hands in it.

Reflect on the experience. Were you able to stay present and observe what you were seeing? Were you distracted? What thoughts came up?

_____

_____

_____

_____

_____

_____

_____

_____

_____

_____

# Mindfulness Meditation

The practices of meditation and mindfulness have many similarities. Both mindfulness and meditation focus on opening the mind and noticing sensations and thoughts without judgment and attachment. Meditation may incorporate mantras, stories, or a dedicated word, event, or phrase. The ideas behind mindfulness and meditation emphasize the concepts of letting go of analysis or overthinking and allowing yourself to follow the natural path of the experience. Some examples of meditative practices include dance, martial arts, moving in nature with your focus on your movement and surroundings, and making music.

What is an activity that you currently engage in that allows you to be completely mindful or meditative? Is there a new activity that you would like to try that would allow you to enter a meditative or mindful practice? How will this improve your quality of life?

_____

_____

_____

_____

_____

_____

_____

_____

_____

_____

_____

_____

_____

_____

_____

_____

_____

_____

_____

_____

_____

_____

_____

_____

# Creating a Mindfulness Routine

Fill in the blanks with your current beliefs about mindfulness meditation.

My current mindfulness meditation practice consists of _____ at least _____ times a _____. I would like to increase my mindfulness meditation practice by adding _____ at least _____ times a _____. I believe that this will help me by _____. Some of my cues for knowing that I need to tune in and practice mindful meditation include:

_____

_____

_____

_____

Creating a mindful meditation plan can help you create awareness when you need to be in tune with your body and be proactive about managing your cues. Having a daily mindful meditation plan can also reduce vulnerability, improve resiliency, and increase connection. Begin mapping out your meditation plan here.

_____

_____

_____

_____

_____

_____

_____

_____

_____

_____

_____

_____

_____

_____

_____

_____

_____

_____

_____

_____

_____

# Tuning in Mindfully

Find a song of any genre to listen to, about three minutes long. Turn off any distractions. Find one instrument or beat to follow for the entirety of the song. Listen to how it fluctuates in rhythm, pace, and tone. Take a break for five minutes, then repeat, following a different instrument. How did the song change? What did you notice about the song each time?

# Three States of Mind

DBT specifies that every person has three states of mind: reasonable mind, emotion mind, and wise mind. Each state of mind has a valuable place in our life. Reasonable mind is the state of mind where we are highly rational, logical, detached, and focused on the facts of an event; emotions have little influence here. Reasonable mind is cool. Emotion mind is when we are highly emotional, reactive, and acting based on emotion, not reason. Emotion mind is hot. Emotion mind and reasonable mind keep us from achieving balance and accessing wise mind. We are either overly withdrawn or overly invested. Wise mind is the balance of reasonable mind and emotion mind. Wise mind accesses our inner wisdom, finds a middle path between reasonable mind and emotion mind, and allows us to access and effectively use our skills to make decisions.

Think about the states of mind. What are situations in your life where you use your reasonable mind? Your emotion mind? Where do you find yourself using your wise mind the most? Are there certain people or situations that make it easier to access certain states of mind? What state of mind is easiest for you to access?

_____

_____

_____

_____

_____

_____

# Feelings within States of Mind

What are some activities, situations, or events that allow you to experience each state of mind (reasonable mind, emotion mind, and wise mind)? How do you know when you are experiencing each state of mind? What tells you that you are in wise mind? What does it feel like when you are in reasonable mind? How do you feel when you are in emotion mind?

_____

_____

_____

_____

_____

_____

_____

_____

_____

_____

_____

_____

_____

_____

# Mindfulness "What" Skills

The "what" skills are used to tell us what we do to practice mindfulness and are meant to be used one at a time; these skills include *observe, describe,* and *participate.*

Observing allows us to notice what is occurring through our senses rather than our thoughts, like walking through a crowded space with our eyes open. Observing is paying attention on purpose. For example, if you're sitting in traffic and another driver cuts you off, rather than being angry, you can observe yourself feeling anger.

Describing involves putting words to the experience you are observing using facts, not interpretations. For example, after you observe that you are feeling angry at the driver who cut you off, you describe the observation: "I'm feeling angry that they just cut me off," or "I'm having the thought that they are a bad driver." You use the describe skill to name the thoughts or feelings you are having when you observe.

Participating is wholeheartedly throwing yourself into an activity without reservation or judgment. Participating allows you to let go of self-consciousness and achieve the highest level of presence in the current moment.

What are some activities, places, or events in your life where you would like to start using the *observe, describe,* and *participate* skills (or start using them more effectively)? How would using these skills change your experience? Is there an activity you have been avoiding that you would like to try while using these skills?

_____

_____

_____

# Flow of Thoughts

As you wake up in the morning, notice the thoughts that arise in your mind. Observe them come and go like waves, allowing them to flow away without attachment. Notice the sensations and thoughts in your body as you release your thoughts. Notice the sensations that come with each thought. How do you feel? Where do you experience each sensation?

_____

_____

_____

_____

_____

_____

_____

_____

_____

_____

_____

_____

_____

# "What" Skills Walk

Go on a walk using the "what" skills without using your cell phone or listening to music. Observe the world around you using your senses. What do you see? What do you smell? Describe the world around you. Is it sunny? Is it cloudy? How does the wind on your face feel? How do the leaves under your feet sound? Participate in the walk and don't try to complete any other activities besides just walking in nature.

_____

_____

_____

_____

_____

_____

_____

_____

_____

_____

_____

_____

# Mindfulness "How" Skills

The "how" skills are our instructions for mindfulness, telling us how to practice the "what" skills: *nonjudgmentally, one-mindfully*, and *effectively*. Our goal in being nonjudgmental is to let go of evaluation while remaining aware of consequences. Evaluations are not facts; they are based upon values and opinions that can cause harm. Contrary to the idea of multi-tasking and accomplishing many things at once, one-mindfully focuses on doing one thing at a time, purposefully and com-pletely as a means of being mindful and present. Effectively focuses on doing what works to meet the goal and letting go of what is "right" or "wrong." In order to be effective, we must know our goal.

How do the judgments that you hold about yourself and others prohibit you from being effective in your personal life? What about at work? How would being nonjudgmental increase your effectiveness in your life? Your relationships? Your work?

# A Life of Gratitude

Think of a time during your life when you were struggling. How did you feel physically during that time? How did you feel mentally during that time? How have you improved? What does your improvement feel like? What does your improvement look like (physically, mentally, financially)?

_____

_____

_____

_____

_____

_____

_____

_____

_____

_____

_____

_____

_____

_____

_____

_____

_____

_____

_____

_____

_____

_____

_____

_____

_____

_____

_____

_____

_____

# Reflect on Your Day Using "How" Skills

Reflect on the activities of your day. What activities did you complete? How effective were you at completing those activities? How could you improve your effectiveness? Were you one-mindful? Were you nonjudgmental of yourself or others? How could you be less judgmental or more one-mindful? What barriers did you encounter while using the "how" skills?

_____

_____

_____

_____

_____

_____

_____

_____

_____

_____

# Taste the "How" Skill

Choose a piece of food, preferably an M&M or a raisin or something similar. Place it in the palm of your hand and observe it, paying attention to its textures and colors. Rub it between your fingers and notice how it feels, noticing the ridges, textures, or smoothness. Be mindful of your judgments and stick to the facts. Now place the food in your mouth. Let your tongue and teeth notice the texture and shape, then bite down. Notice the sound. Does the taste change? Does the texture change? Describe the experience. Were you able to describe the food without judgment? Were you able to be one-mindful during this experience? Do you think you were effective?

_____

_____

_____

_____

_____

_____

_____

_____

_____

# Observing Thoughts Skill

In 2020, researchers at Queen's University discovered that we have about 6,200 thoughts per day on average. We do not recognize all those thoughts because we are not observing or mindful of all our thoughts that occur throughout the day. Incorporating "how" and "what" skills allows us to observe our thoughts without judgment and accept them as they are. By observing our thoughts, we can allow them to come and go without attachment or trying to change them, observing them as if they were objects on the side of the road as we drive by.

What power do your thoughts have over your choices and decisions when you allow them to have judgment? How would you feel if you took away the judgment and value behind those thoughts and just allowed them to be thoughts? What if your judgmental thoughts were just words on a screen, without meaning; how would that change how you feel about yourself?

_____

_____

_____

_____

_____

_____

_____

_____

# Thoughts as Waves

As you prepare for bed, get comfortable and allow your thoughts to come and go as waves on the beach, each coming and going, leaving shells of knowledge for you. Without attaching to your thoughts, notice the sensations in your body as you observe each thought coming and going. What sensations do you notice arise with each thought? Where do you feel the sensations? Do some thoughts and sensations feel better than others?

_____

_____

_____

_____

_____

_____

_____

_____

_____

_____

_____

_____

# Wordless Watching of Thoughts

Lay down somewhere comfortable and close your eyes. As thoughts begin to arise, watch as they enter and leave your mind. Label each time a thought enters your mind as "A thought has entered my mind," and each time the thought leaves, "A thought has left my mind." Do not attach judgment to the types of thoughts that enter or exit. How does it feel for you to just observe your thoughts without judgment? Do you notice tension? Relief? Fear?

_____

_____

_____

_____

_____

_____

_____

_____

_____

_____

# Sensing Mindfully

During a chaotic moment, give yourself space to focus on the things around you that you don't usually notice. Find awareness of five things you can smell, five things you can hear, five things you can feel, five things you can taste, and five things you can see. Describe each of these things without judgment. How does this awareness reduce your suffering? How does this reduce your feelings of chaos and anxiety? What other times in your life might this be helpful to use?

_____

_____

_____

_____

_____

_____

_____

_____

_____

_____

_____

_____

# Getting a Feel for Mindfulness

Find somewhere comfortable to sit. Notice the feel of the seat on your back, on your legs, and your weight in the chair. Inhale through your nose, letting the air fill your lungs and travel to your belly. Take a few more deep breaths. Notice the air coming into your nose; how does it feel? How does the air feel in your throat? In your lungs? In your belly? How does it feel to focus on your breath coming in and out of your body? Where do you notice your thoughts drifting?

_____

_____

_____

_____

_____

_____

_____

_____

_____

_____

*I am releasing judgment and accepting peace.*

# PART TWO

# Distress Tolerance: Deal with Upsetting Emotions and Control Impulses

In this section, we will explore prompts and exercises focused on distress tolerance and how these skills help in reducing symptoms of BPD. We will expand on the following skills: check the facts, cope ahead, the STOP skill, self-soothing with five senses, reality acceptance skills, IMPROVE the moment, and managing impulsive urges. These skills are meant to help you manage crises or situations in the short term, but should not be used to assist you in reaching long-term goals. Feel free to read over "Core Principle 2: Distress Tolerance" on page xi for a refresher on what distress tolerance is as you work through this section.

# Check the Facts

Borderline personality disorder is often associated with a certain type of thought called a cognitive distortion. Cognitive distortions are negative, irrational, and inaccurate thoughts. For many with BPD, cognitive distortions can lead to strong emotions and big reactions. For example, your partner doesn't return your text message for a while and you automatically think they don't want to be with you anymore. This irrational thought causes you to feel sad and angry, and you send them countless texts accusing them of dumping you. But then you get a call from your partner a few hours later—they tell you they were in a meeting at work and didn't get your messages until now, and they're confused about why they would be dumping you and why you're acting this way. In this example, the cognitive distortion could be "If my partner doesn't return my messages right away, it means they don't love me and want to leave me." Cognitive distortions and fears around abandonment are common experiences associated with BPD. Check the facts is a skill for challenging these cognitive distortions, helping you change unwanted emotions by looking at the facts instead of allowing your perceptions to take over.

With this skill, we'll focus on becoming aware of the facts of a situation, not our perceptions of a situation. A fact is something that is known or has been proven to be true. First, identify the emotion you want to change. Next, identify the situation that led to this emotional response. Create a list of assumptions you have about the situation. Are you assuming there is a threat, like being abandoned in the example? If your emotions fit with the facts of the situation, use your distress tolerance skills. If the facts do not fit, explore and problem-solve a response that would be more appropriate.

Our perception of situations or relationships can lead to an altered perception of reality. Think back to a recent situation where you experienced cognitive distortions about a situation or a relationship, ones that were not based on fact. How could checking the facts improve or change the outcome of this situation? How could checking the facts impact your feelings about the situation?

_____

_____

_____

_____

_____

_____

_____

_____

_____

_____

_____

_____

# Check the Facts When Your Perceptions Are Misleading

When have you based your behaviors on a cognitive distortion? When have your perceptions of a situation led you in the opposite direction of the truth? What was your perception of the situation? What was the outcome? How did your actions impact your relationships? What were the facts of the situation? What can you do to catch yourself in the future and avoid acting on perception instead of checking the facts before you act?

_____

_____

_____

_____

_____

_____

_____

_____

_____

_____

_____

_____

# Checking the Facts Step-by-Step

Try checking the facts for a situation you are dealing with. What's the emotion you want to change? What event prompted your emotion? What are your interpretations about the event? Are you creating a threat or catastrophe? Do your emotions fit the facts?

Emotion:

_____

Prompting Event:

_____

Interpretations:

_____

Threat/Catastrophe:

_____

Facts:

_____

_____

_____

Do my emotions fit the facts? (Circle one)   **Yes   No**
Next steps? Use distress tolerance skills or change my emotions to fit the facts.

# STOP Skill

This skill is helpful in managing and stopping impulsive actions associated with BPD, like lashing out at others or engaging in dangerous acts. STOP stands for **S**top, **T**ake a step back, **O**bserve, and **P**roceed mindfully. It is best to use this skill when you feel like your emotions are about to take over. When using this skill, physically freeze—DO NOT MOVE! You are in control of your emotions and your body. Remove yourself from the situation and observe what is going on for you, physically and emotionally, as well as what is going on for others. Remember to gather facts, not perceptions. Now, proceed mindfully after you feel confident in your ability to move forward.

Where do you foresee using the STOP skill most? Is it at work, school, with your friends, with your family? What aspect of this skill do you imagine being most difficult to use? What are some simple ways or situations to practice this skill?

_____

_____

_____

_____

_____

_____

_____

# Using STOP in Relationships

How do you see yourself using this skill in the future with your relationships? What recent relationship conflicts have you encountered where this skill would have been helpful? How would using this skill change a situation? How would you use this skill in these types of conflicts moving forward?

_____

_____

_____

_____

_____

_____

_____

_____

_____

_____

_____

_____

_____

_____

_____

_____

_____

_____

_____

_____

_____

_____

_____

_____

_____

_____

_____

_____

_____

# Practicing STOP Step-by-Step

It's Monday morning and you're waiting in line at your favorite coffee shop, which also happens to be very busy this morning. Someone else in the store is talking on their phone and they cut in front of you. Use the STOP skill to manage your reaction to this situation and keep the situation from ruining your day.

Stop:

_____

_____

_____

Take a step back:

_____

_____

_____

Observe:

_____

_____

Proceed mindfully:

_____

_____

# Self-Soothing with Five Senses

Self-soothing can be difficult when you are at a high level of distress. This skill focuses on simple, easily accessible ways to self-soothe using your five senses to decrease distress. The purpose of this is to do something pleasant or comforting to provide relief from pain or stress as a means of passing time without increasing distress or misery. This skill is meant to provide comfort, peace, and kindness by using sight, smell, taste, touch, and sound. Self-soothing does not endorse damage to the body. If you lack access to one or more of your senses, please use what senses you have access to for this exercise.

Thinking back throughout your life, what has brought you comfort and peace in times of pain, sadness, or sickness? How can you recreate that thing or feeling to bring yourself comfort in the current moment? Is there an image, smell, taste, sound, or touch that you associate with this comfort? If this is a new idea for you, what would you like to associate with peace and comfort? Is it a smell, a taste, a color, a picture, a sound, or a texture?

_____

_____

_____

_____

_____

_____

_____

---

---

---

---

---

---

---

---

---

---

---

---

---

---

---

---

---

---

# Exploring Your Favorite Senses

Think about your favorite taste and describe how it tastes when it is perfect. How does it make you feel? What does it make you think of?

_____

_____

_____

_____

_____

   Think about a smell that you enjoy and describe the smell. What does it remind you of? How do you feel when you smell it?

_____

_____

_____

_____

_____

Think of your favorite texture. How does it feel? How do you feel when you touch it? What do you think about when you touch it?

_____

_____

_____

_____

_____

_____

Think of your favorite image or picture, and describe the image. How do you feel when you think of the image? What do you associate with this image?

_____

_____

_____

_____

_____

_____

# Practice Using Your Senses

In times of heightened distress, it can be hard to access your skills to manage or decrease the crisis. Find a small bag or pouch and gather a few items that utilize your five senses and will help calm you or lower your distress during a crisis. Keep this kit with you or make multiple kits for home, work, school, etc. Write down objects to gather below. Examples can include pictures of animals or loved ones, headphones, sour candy, or essential oil.

If you lack access to one or more of your senses, please use what senses you have access to for this exercise.

Sight:

_____

Smell:

_____

Taste:

_____

Touch:

_____

Sound:

_____

# Reality Acceptance Skills

When dealing with a diagnosis of BPD, it can be a challenge to accept difficult emotions. Reality acceptance skills focus on reducing suffering and increasing freedom. There are six reality acceptance skills: radical acceptance, turning the mind, willingness, half-smiling, willing hands, and mindfulness of current thoughts. However, in this book we will focus only on radical acceptance, willingness, and willing hands. Radical acceptance is a helpful skill for accepting feelings, people, events, and facts just as they are. Radical acceptance is not approval, justification, or validation; it is simply accepting the things that you cannot change. Other resources for these skills can be found in the *DBT Skills Training Manual* (Linehan, 2015).

Radical acceptance is complete acceptance of a situation, idea, or feeling. Keep in mind that acceptance is not approval. One can accept something difficult without approving of it. It is helpful to recognize radical acceptance as a complete and thorough acknowledgment of the unchangeable facts. Radical acceptance is often something that takes practice and revisiting before it sticks.

Willingness is acceptance and readiness to participate and do just what is needed in each given moment, mindfully and without hesitation or resentment. When acting willingly, one is acting from their wise mind and with awareness. Willingness is the opposite of willfulness. Willfulness refuses to tolerate or be present in the current moment and insists on being in control.

Imagine accepting something small, like having to wake up early, without having anger or resentment, lashing out, or harming yourself. Sit or lie with your eyes closed for a few moments while imagining this. What thoughts or feelings come up? What sensations do you notice? What was difficult? Easy?

_____

_____

_____

_____

_____

_____

_____

_____

_____

_____

_____

_____

_____

_____

_____

_____

# Willingness in Difficult Situations

Think about a current situation or feeling in your life that you are being willful about. What are you doing that is willful? What can you do to be more willing with the situation? How would having willingness help you improve the situation or reduce suffering? How would being willing improve the overall outcome of the situation?

_____

_____

_____

_____

_____

_____

_____

_____

_____

_____

_____

_____

_____

_____

_____

_____

_____

_____

_____

_____

_____

_____

_____

_____

_____

_____

_____

_____

_____

_____

_____

# Willing Hands: Accepting Reality with Your Body

For about a minute, while sitting down, place your hands palms up on top of your lap. Relax your hands and unclench your fists. This posture tells your brain that you are open and ready to receive energy. Use this skill to release willfulness and accept willingness into your body and mind. Try this skill in different situations to let go of stress and tense energy. Try it in traffic, while having a difficult conversation, while doing a task you don't enjoy, or first thing in the morning.

_____

_____

_____

_____

_____

_____

_____

_____

_____

# IMPROVE the Moment

As we continue to explore ways to reduce distress and manage crises related to symptoms and situations associated with BPD, this skill looks to incorporate things such as **I**magery, **M**eaning, **P**rayer, **R**elaxation, **O**ne thing in the moment, **V**acation, and self-**E**ncouragement (IMPROVE).

The goal of **I**magery is to imagine being in a calming, peaceful place to help promote relaxation and calming feelings. The goal of **M**eaning is to find meaning in painful events, listen to spiritual values, or find spiritual values to hold close for the purpose of strength. **P**rayer is meant to open your heart and mind to your higher power, give things over to your higher power, or ask for strength. **R**elaxation is for promoting self-care and relaxing actions, such as taking a warm bath, massaging your neck, practicing yoga, or breathing deeply. **O**ne thing in the moment brings awareness to mindfulness, recentering yourself in the moment and focusing your entire attention on one thing at a time. **V**acation allows you to take a brief break from things, with the intention of returning later. Give yourself a brief vacation, take a nap, go for a drive, turn off your phone for the day, or take a 1-hour break from work. Self-**E**ncouragement is meant to help you rethink the situation or cheerlead yourself with positive statements and affirmations.

Which components of IMPROVE are you using currently? Which components do you need to work on? When are you using this skill the most? How can you plan to use the components of this skill that need to be improved upon over the next week? Commit to trying each component at least twice per week. Note the difference in how you feel after.

_____

_____

_____

_____

_____

_____

_____

_____

_____

_____

_____

_____

_____

_____

_____

_____

_____

_____

_____

_____

# Reflecting on IMPROVE

After one week of practicing this skill, think about where you used it the most. Was it at work? At home? Socially? What aspects of these situations are requiring you to use this skill? Are there things about these situations that you can change to reduce your emotional reaction in the long term?

_____

_____

_____

_____

_____

_____

_____

_____

_____

_____

_____

_____

_____

_____

_____

_____

_____

_____

_____

_____

_____

_____

_____

_____

_____

_____

_____

_____

# IMPROVE Practice

Now that you've had practice with IMPROVE, focus on upcoming stressors that you can anticipate and write out a plan for improving the moment. What is the stressor? What will be the most helpful responses?

_____

_____

Imagery:

_____

Meaning:

_____

Prayer:

_____

Relaxation:

_____

One thing in the moment:

_____

Vacation:

_____

Self-Encouragement:

_____

# Managing Impulsivity

Impulsivity can be a difficult but common problem to manage when dealing with BPD. Impulsivity in BPD is an emotionally driven behavior that may have harmful consequences. Examples can include impulsive sexual behavior, shoplifting, spending money, using drugs, binge drinking, driving fast, or self-injury. Impulsivity can be spurred by intense pain that cannot be relieved quickly, acting from emotion mind, threats of emotional distress worsening, crises creating pressure, feeling overwhelmed, needing to meet the needs or demands of yourself or others, having extreme arousal, and having problems that cannot be handled immediately.

It's important to note that impulsivity can also stem from other psychological and physiological needs. DBT pros and cons, the STOP skill, the TIPP skill, distracting, and self-soothing are excellent resources for managing and recovering from impulse urges. We will explore the use of the TIPP skill, the STOP skill, and pros and cons to address impulsivity.

When do you find yourself struggling with impulsivity? Are there certain people that trigger you to be more impulsive? Are there certain stressors that trigger impulsivity (money, pain, illness)? What is your thought process around your impulsivity? How do you feel before you are impulsive? How do you feel after?

_____

_____

_____

_____

# Reflecting on Impulsivity

If you could be given the superpower to change something about your impulsivity, what would you change? What do you dislike most about your impulsivity? What do you like most about it? How does your impulsivity hurt your relationships with those around you?

_____

_____

_____

_____

_____

_____

_____

_____

_____

_____

_____

_____

_____

_____

_____

_____

_____

_____

_____

_____

_____

_____

_____

_____

_____

_____

_____

_____

# Managing Impulsivity with STOP

Distress tolerance skills, like the STOP skill, are also useful for avoiding impulsive actions. Think about a situation that could trigger an impulsive response in the future and visualize applying the STOP skill to your potential reaction. **S**top, **T**ake a step back (physically remove yourself from the situation), **O**bserve what is going on around you and within you, and **P**roceed mindfully. This skill allows for you to slow down and evaluate the environment and how you feel before proceeding.

Situation:

_____

Stop:

_____

_____

Take a step back:

_____

_____

Observe what is going on:

_____

Proceed mindfully:

_____

# TIPP Skill

The TIPP skill stands for **T**ip the temperature of your face with cold water, **I**ntense exercise for 15 minutes, **P**aced breathing, and **P**aired muscle relaxation. These skills, when used alone or together, can help reduce emotion mind and calm you when you are at a skills breakdown point. They can also help when you're not processing information correctly, when you are in an emotional crisis, or when you are too overwhelmed to make a decision.

The TIPP skill is a central nervous system reset. Thinking back on your crisis urges and impulsive behaviors, when would a reset like this be helpful for managing your behavior and avoiding making things worse? When do you see yourself using this skill in the future? What can you do to remember to use this skill? Where can you leave reminders for yourself?

_____

_____

_____

_____

_____

_____

_____

_____

_____

_____

_____

_____

_____

_____

_____

_____

_____

_____

_____

_____

_____

_____

_____

_____

_____

_____

# Paced Breathing Practice

Find a comfortable place to lie down and bring your attention to your breath. Breathe in through your nose for four seconds. Breathe out through your mouth for six seconds. Repeat this for about two minutes. What sensations did you notice while practicing? Did you notice any changes in your emotional arousal level? How did it feel to just focus on your breathing?

---

---

---

---

---

---

---

---

---

---

---

---

# Pros and Cons of Acting on Impulse

Identify an impulse behavior you have engaged in. What are the advantages and disadvantages of participating in the behavior? What are the short-term consequences? What are the long-term consequences? What are the pros of acting on the impulse? What are the cons of acting on the impulse?

_____

_____

_____

_____

_____

_____

_____

_____

_____

_____

_____

_____

_____

_____

_____

_____

_____

_____

_____

_____

_____

_____

_____

_____

_____

_____

_____

_____

# Pros and Cons Exercise

Complete a pros and cons list for a recurrent impulsive behavior that you struggle with. After completing the chart, take a picture and keep it with you to consult when you're struggling with the impulse in the future. Keep in mind short-term and long-term consequences.

Impulsive behavior: _____

|  | ACTING ON BEHAVIOR | RESISTING BEHAVIOR |
|---|---|---|
| PROS |  |  |
| CONS |  |  |

*I am strong and capable of overcoming difficult feelings.*

# PART THREE

# Emotion Regulation: Understand Your Feelings and Express Them in a Healthy Way

In this section, we will explore exercises, prompts, and affirmations related to emotion regulation skills and how these skills can help reduce intense emotions and symptoms of BPD. We will expand on the following skills: opposite action, problem-solving, ABC, PLEASE, cope ahead, mindfulness of current emotions, and managing extreme emotions. These skills are used to understand and name your emotions while decreasing unwanted emotions, emotional vulnerability, and emotional suffering. Feel free to reread "Core Principle 3: Emotion Regulation" on page xii for a refresher on what emotion regulation is as you work through this section.

# Opposite Action

Opposite action is, very simply, acting opposite of your emotional urges. This is the second step of check the facts, which you practiced earlier in this workbook. Often with BPD, you may have an elevated emotional response to an experience—a response that may not be appropriate for the situation. In these moments when you would like to reduce your suffering or change an unwanted emotion or response, opposite action can be very effective. It is also helpful when your emotional intensity or duration is not effective for meeting your goals and when you are engaging in avoiding behaviors. Practice opposite action by naming the emotion you want to change, checking the facts of the situation, identifying your action urge, and then acting opposite of your emotional urge.

Think of an intense emotion that tends to show up for you frequently or causes you a lot of distress. Does that emotion fit the facts of the situation when it presents itself? If it doesn't fit, what are some ways that you can act opposite of the emotion? Remember to act opposite all the way, not just a little bit, for this skill to work.

_____

_____

_____

_____

_____

_____

# Don't Feed the Impulse Monster

Opposite action can be helpful for impulsivity. What is an impulsive action that tends to be problematic for you? What are your triggers or red flags that appear before you engage in this behavior? Use these warning signs as cues to act opposite to prevent the impulsive behavior. Remember to see the opposite action all the way through to the end for the skill to be most effective.

_____

_____

_____

_____

_____

_____

_____

_____

_____

_____

_____

_____

_____

_____

_____

_____

_____

_____

_____

_____

_____

_____

_____

_____

_____

_____

_____

_____

# Identifying Opposite Actions

Below is a list of common emotions and the action that typically fits the facts associated with them. In the space provided,
name the opposite emotion and behavior that fit the facts.

Love (approach). Opposite emotions and action:

_____

Anger (attack). Opposite emotions and action:

_____

Shame (hide). Opposite emotions and action:

_____

Sadness (isolate). Opposite emotions and action:

_____

Fear (run away). Opposite emotions and action:

_____

_____

_____

_____

_____

# Cope Ahead

Cope ahead is a skill used to anticipate stressful or distressing situations, creating a plan in advance that will allow you to effectively cope with stressors. Part of the plan involves imagining yourself in the situation and seeing yourself coping effectively. This skill requires describing the problem or situation, deciding on what skills to use, imagining the situation, and then rehearsing the coping skill in your mind before trying it out in real life.

What is an event or situation that tends to cause you a high level of emotional dysregulation or distress? What about the event causes this reaction for you? Is it the people? Is it the environment? If you could change one thing about the situation, what would it be? Now imagine yourself participating successfully. What would that look like? What would that feel like? Write a step-by-step plan for managing the event or situation successfully.

_____

_____

_____

_____

_____

_____

_____

_____

# Controlled Chaos

Thinking about a difficult event or situation, what is the story you would like to be able to tell for how you managed and succeeded? Write a story for how you went to an event that is difficult for you and succeeded using the cope ahead skill.

_____

_____

_____

_____

_____

_____

_____

_____

_____

_____

_____

_____

_____

_____

_____

_____

_____

_____

_____

_____

_____

_____

_____

_____

_____

_____

_____

_____

_____

_____

# Practicing Cope Ahead

Write out a cope ahead plan for an upcoming event or situation that you have concerns about.

What are you concerned about?

_____

_____

What is the worst thing that you imagine happening?

_____

_____

How do you imagine coping with the worst-case scenario?

_____

_____

What is your plan for self-care before and after the situation/event?

_____

_____

How did the event/situation go? Were you successful in managing it? Rate your distress level (0 to 10):

Before? _____ During? _____ After? _____

# ABC

The ABC skills are used to help you become less vulnerable to painful emotions over time. ABC stands for **A**ccumulate positive emotions, **B**uild mastery, and **C**ope ahead of time. When you continue to practice and experience positive emotions, you are less susceptible to negative emotions taking control of your life. ABC allows you to create positive experiences on a regular basis, enabling you to have a higher threshold for negative emotions. Building mastery means practicing tasks or activities that make you feel capable and confident in your abilities, reducing your feelings of hopelessness and helplessness. And as previously discussed, using the cope ahead skill allows you to be prepared to handle difficult situations before they occur.

Reflect on three things in your life that you have been avoiding over the last six months. How does this avoidance align with your values and priorities? How is this contributing to your short-term and long-term goals?

---

---

---

---

---

---

---

How would adding two positive events into your weekly routine increase the amount of joy you experience? If finances and time were not barriers, what two activities would you add to your weekly routine? With the resources that you have, how can you incorporate these activities into your life?

_____

_____

_____

_____

_____

_____

_____

_____

_____

_____

_____

_____

# Build Mastery

Explore a few actions that would help you stop avoiding the activities you listed in the ABC prompt on page 86. Brainstorm small action steps you can take. What activities can you practice that would help you meet your goals? How would building mastery over these activities improve your life?

_____

_____

_____

_____

_____

_____

_____

_____

_____

_____

_____

_____

_____

_____

_____

_____

_____

_____

_____

_____

_____

_____

_____

_____

_____

_____

_____

_____

_____

_____

_____

_____

# Avoid Avoiding

What are some of the tasks or activities in your life that you have been avoiding? What is contributing to you avoiding these activities? Is delaying these activities preventing you from reaching your short-term or long-term goals? What are one or two action steps you could take this week to help you stop avoiding and start acting opposite? How would this improve your life?

_____

_____

_____

_____

_____

_____

_____

_____

_____

_____

_____

# Practicing ABC

Practice accumulating positive events each day:

| DAY | ONE POSITIVE EVENT EACH DAY RELATED TO SHORT-TERM GOALS | ONE POSITIVE EVENT EACH DAY RELATED TO LONG-TERM GOALS | ONE POSITIVE EVENT EACH DAY RELATED TO AVOIDING AVOIDING |
|---|---|---|---|
| M | | | |
| T | | | |
| W | | | |
| T | | | |
| F | | | |
| S | | | |
| S | | | |

Practice building mastery each day:

| DAY | ONE EVENT EACH DAY TO BUILD YOUR SENSE OF ACCOMPLISHMENT | ONE EVENT EACH DAY THAT IS DIFFICULT BUT ACHIEVABLE |
|---|---|---|
| M | | |
| T | | |
| W | | |
| T | | |
| F | | |
| S | | |
| S | | |

# PLEASE

The PLEASE skill focuses on supporting a healthy body so you can support a healthy mind. PLEASE stands for:

**treating PhysicaL illness:** Being sick or in pain lowers your threshold for emotional discomfort. Treat any physical illnesses you have as prescribed as a means of reducing emotional vulnerability.

**balanced Eating:** Eating routinely and eating food that makes you feel good can help reduce emotional vulnerability. Eating too much, eating too little, or eating the wrong things can all contribute to emotional vulnerability.

**Avoiding mood-altering substances:** The use of illicit drugs and alcohol can lead to impulsive behaviors and increase emotional vulnerability. Avoid these substances in order to stay in wise mind.

**balanced Sleep:** It is recommended that adults get between seven and nine hours of sleep per night for optimal brain functioning and health. Good sleep hygiene, routine, and sleep habits are ideal for reducing emotional vulnerability and increasing time spent feeling good.

**Exercise:** Consistent aerobic exercise is often viewed as an antidepressant. Try to move your body a little bit every day to increase feelings of joy and increase mastery.

What lessons have you learned from not following the PLEASE skill? How does your body respond to not treating physical illness? Not eating well? Consuming drugs or alcohol? Not sleeping enough? Not exercising or moving your body? How does your mood respond?

_____

_____

_____

_____

_____

_____

_____

_____

_____

_____

_____

_____

_____

# Creating a Balanced Life

How can you create limits and buffers for yourself within your life to manage what you need using the **PLEASE** skill? Think about how much exercise, sleep, calories, hydration, and movement you need each day in order to feel like the best version of yourself. What does that look like? How can you fit that in while having a job? A social life?

_____

_____

_____

_____

_____

_____

_____

_____

_____

_____

_____

_____

_____

# Sleep Log

Sleep hygiene is a large part of making sure your mental health is managed. Maintaining a sleep hygiene log for one week can help you begin to manage the challenges associated with getting good sleep.

| DAY | HOURS OF SLEEP | OUNCES OF CAFFEINE | OUNCES OF ALCOHOL | SCREEN TIME | QUALITY OF SLEEP (1–10) |
|---|---|---|---|---|---|
| M | | | | | |
| T | | | | | |
| W | | | | | |
| T | | | | | |
| F | | | | | |
| S | | | | | |
| S | | | | | |

# Mindfulness of Current Emotions

To build on our use of mindfulness, we can use this skill to let go of emotional suffering. Mindfulness of current emotions is practiced by observing your emotions, taking notice of them and allowing the experience, and letting the feelings come and go like waves on the beach. Do not try and block anything from coming. Remember that the feeling will not last forever. Do not hold onto the feeling, do not push it away, and do not inflate or magnify it.

Notice where in your body you feel the emotion. Observe how long the sensation lasts. You are not your emotions. Feelings are temporary sensations of your mind. Practice respecting your feelings, but do not judge them. Try to radically accept them.

_____

_____

_____

_____

_____

_____

_____

_____

_____

_____

_____

_____

_____

_____

_____

_____

_____

_____

_____

_____

_____

_____

_____

# Releasing Emotions

Notice a time when you are feeling frustrated, angry, sad, lonely, or shameful. Have a conversation out loud with yourself detailing how you feel. Name the emotions you are experiencing, both physically and mentally. What do you notice as you release these feelings from your body? How does it feel to acknowledge your feelings? What sensations do you notice? Do you notice a sense of relief? A sense of shame?

# Inventory of Emotions

At the beginning of your day, start your day with an inventory of your emotions. What do you feel? Do you have residual feelings from yesterday? What sensations do you notice in your body? Are they associated with your feelings? Remember not to judge these feelings or push them away. Sit with these feelings for two minutes. Get comfortable with how they feel and how they make your body feel.

_____

_____

_____

_____

_____

_____

_____

_____

_____

_____

# Managing Extreme Emotions

A high level of distress can signify a skills breakdown point, a time in which skills may not be as effective for you. Trouble-shooting your distress to get back on track may be helpful as a means of effectively regulating your emotions and not acting impulsively. These feelings may occur in certain situations or around certain people. Learning these cues can help you manage and reduce your distress. Here are some things to be mindful of when looking out for extreme emotions:

Observe your distress:

- Your distress is extreme.

- You are feeling overwhelmed.

- Your emotions are distracting in their intensity.

- Your ability to problem-solve is limited.

Reflect on a time when your emotions were extreme. What was going on in your life that led up to this? Were you overwhelmed at work? Were you physically ill? Were you experiencing pain? Had you been sleeping enough? What can you do in the future to avoid experiencing extreme emotions? How can you manage extreme emotions when they arise?

_____

_____

_____

_____

_____

# Managing Emotional Overload

Are there people or situations in your life that tend to make you experience more extreme emotions? What about them makes your emotions feel extreme? How can you prepare for these situations and manage your emotions to avoid reaching these extremes?

---

Think back to the last time you experienced extreme emotions. What signs tell you that you are at the point of emotional overload? Do you get a feeling in your body (shaking, turning red, a pit in your stomach, a headache)? What do your emotions feel like when you are at your capacity? Do you have trouble thinking clearly?

_____

_____

_____

_____

_____

_____

_____

_____

_____

_____

_____

_____

# Managing Extreme Emotions with Skills

When experiencing extreme emotions, run through a quick checklist for yourself to problem-solve and get back on track! Ask yourself the following questions:

Am I managing my biological sensitivities? Have I eaten? Have I slept enough? Am I in pain? Have I taken my prescribed medication?

- Work on your PLEASE skill.
  - Try ABC skills.

Have I used my skills? Am I using my skills effectively? Make sure you are following your skills all the way to completion.

- Distress tolerance skills are very effective in these times.
- Get coaching if your skills aren't working.
- Try again!

What are your emotions telling you?

- Are they motivating you?
- Are they communicating a message to others?
- Do they validate your beliefs and feelings?
  - Try pros and cons.
  - Try opposite action.
  - Practice self-validation.
  - Practice radical acceptance and willingness.

What is your emotional overload like? Are you too upset to problem-solve?

- Try using the TIPP skill for a reset.

  - Use other distress tolerance skills for managing the crisis.

_____

_____

_____

_____

_____

_____

_____

_____

_____

_____

_____

_____

*I am deserving of peace and positivity.*

# PART FOUR

# Interpersonal Effectiveness: Assert Your Needs and Manage Conflict

In this section, we will explore exercises, prompts, and affirmations related to interpersonal effectiveness and how these skills help in managing relationships when dealing with the symptoms and feelings associated with BPD. We will expand on the following skills: priorities within relationships, DEAR MAN, GIVE, FAST, validation, the drama triangle, and ending relationships. These skills are used for managing and maintaining your interpersonal relationships, making new friends, and making decisions related to your relationships. Take another look at "Core Principle 4: Interpersonal Effectiveness" on page xiii for a refresher on what interpersonal effectiveness is as you work through this section.

# Priorities within Relationships

Throughout the various relationships in your life, you will encounter different types of conflicts that push you to focus on different priorities. These priorities can range from self-respect to the relationship itself to an objective (doing what you feel is right). But no matter *what* your priority is in the given situation, it's important to be aware of it as a means of knowing your goal. It's also important to not let problems build, to know why you are engaging in the conflict, and to know the result or change you would like to see.

There are different priorities that you can use to manage your approach to conflict. Objective effectiveness refers to meeting a specific goal or attaining a certain outcome from the interaction. This type of effectiveness focuses on the outcome or change instead of feelings. Relationship effectiveness refers to maintaining or improving the relationship; the goal is to strengthen or keep the relationship. Self-respect effectiveness refers to improving your feelings about yourself and your values and morals.

Think of a current conflict or conversation that you are engaged in with a friend, family member, or peer. How would identifying your priorities improve the communication, as well as improve how you handle the conversation? How do you want to feel about the communication? How do you want the other person to feel?

---

---

---

---

_____

_____

_____

_____

_____

_____

_____

_____

_____

_____

_____

_____

_____

_____

_____

_____

# Improving Communication

Think about a conversation that you need to have but have been avoiding. Would clarifying your priorities help you stop avoiding the conversation? How would identifying your priorities improve the communication? Think about each of the priorities: the objective, the relationship, and self-respect. Which of those is most important to you in this current conversation? What makes it most important?

_____

_____

_____

_____

_____

_____

_____

_____

_____

_____

# Planning a Relationship Conversation

Plan for a conversation you need to have. Think about your priorities within the conversation. Rate your priorities and describe your goals for each priority. Explain how you want to feel and how you want the other person to feel about you and the conversation.

**Objective:**

_____

_____

How I want to feel:

_____

_____

How I want them to feel:

_____

_____

**Relationship:**

_____

_____

How I want to feel:

_____

_____

How I want them to feel:

_____

_____

**Self-Respect:**

_____

_____

How I want to feel:

_____

_____

How I want them to feel:

_____

_____

# DEAR MAN Skill

Upon clarifying your priority within a situation, it's important to be skillful in asking for what you need or want from another person or group. The DEAR MAN skill allows you to be skillful and mindful in asking with intention.

**D**escribe the current situation.

**E**xpress your feelings about the situation using "I feel" statements.

**A**ssert yourself by asking for what you want or need, or by saying no to a request.

**R**einforce the positive or negative consequences of the other person's behavior ahead of time.

Stay **M**indful of your goal. Ignore attacks and repeat your requests, or say no if you find you are repeating yourself too much without progress.

**A**ppear confident and effective, use a strong voice, and make eye contact.

**N**egotiate. Be willing to give or problem-solve to get what you need.

Think about a request you need to make of someone that you have been avoiding. Why have you been avoiding making this request? Do you have the skills to make the request? Can the other person give you what you are requesting? Is it appropriate within your relationship to make this request? How can you use the DEAR MAN skill to guide you in making this request without using manipulation or threatening tactics?

_____

_____

_____

_____

_____

_____

_____

_____

_____

_____

_____

_____

_____

_____

_____

_____

_____

_____

# Preparing to Skillfully Say No

Think about something you've recently committed to or been asked to do that you don't want to do. Why are you reluctant to commit to or engage in the request? Is the request appropriate for your relationship? Do you owe the person a favor? Do you have the skills to say no? Do you have the ability to commit to or engage in the request? How could using the DEAR MAN skill allow you to skillfully say no without manipulation, lies, or causing harm to the relationship?

_____

_____

_____

_____

_____

_____

_____

_____

_____

_____

_____

_____

_____

---

---

---

---

---

---

---

---

---

---

---

---

---

# Practicing DEAR MAN

Think of an upcoming difficult conversation or request and use DEAR MAN to prepare you to navigate the conversation you would like to have.

Describe:

_____

Express:

_____

Assert:

_____

Reinforce:

_____

(Stay) Mindful:

_____

Appear confident:

_____

Negotiate:

_____

# GIVE Skill

The GIVE skill goes hand in hand with the DEAR MAN and FAST skills. This skill is meant to inform your tone and body language when communicating with others during tough conversations.

**(Be) Gentle:** Be respectful with your words and actions. No physical or verbal attacks. Keep a calm, gentle body language and tone.

**(Act) Interested:** Listen without judgment and show interest in what the other person has to say. Listen to the other person's point of view. Make eye contact and face the person while listening to them.

**Validate:** Use your words and your body language to show that you are understanding of the other person's feelings and thoughts. Briefly put yourself in their shoes.

**(Use an) Easy manner:** Light humor never hurt to lighten the mood of a heavy conversation. Use a smile and a calm tone of voice. A calm and gentle manner is best here.

Thinking back to previous conflicts or communication in your relationships, where have you struggled most? How has this impacted your relationships? How can you use the GIVE skill to improve your communication? Which part of the GIVE skill could you improve in the most?

_____

_____

# Effective Communication Skills

Think about a conflict you had with someone recently. How could using the GIVE skill improve your communication with them? What part of the GIVE skill were you missing? Do you think this made the communication worse or better? How can you remember to use this skill in future interactions to avoid repeating the error?

_____

_____

_____

_____

_____

_____

_____

_____

_____

_____

_____

_____

_____

_____

_____

_____

_____

_____

_____

_____

_____

_____

_____

_____

_____

_____

_____

_____

# FAST Skill

The FAST skill continues to build on the DEAR MAN and GIVE skills. Where the GIVE skill helps in maintaining respect for the other person, the FAST skill helps in maintain self-respect.

**(Be) Fair:** Be fair to yourself and the other person involved. Remember to validate your own thoughts and feelings, as well as those of the other person. Your feelings and thoughts about the conversation are just as valid as the other person's.

**(No) Apologies:** Do not *over* apologize. Do not make an apology for being alive, making a request, disagreeing, or having a different opinion. Do not carry shame in your body or face. Do not invalidate any valid thoughts or feelings of yourself or others.

**Stick to your values:** Do not degrade your morals or values based on someone else's opinion. Be clear about what you believe in. Act and speak based on your morals and values. Do not waver based upon what the other person is saying. Stick to your guns.

**(Be) Truthful:** Do not lie or make up stories. Do not exaggerate or tell the other person what you think they what to hear. Do not make up excuses. Stick to the facts.

When reflecting on previous communications, how has your use of the FAST skill been lacking? What does that lack look like in your communication? What consequences does that result in for your communication? How can you improve in

using the FAST skill? How do you think using this skill regularly
will improve your communication outcomes?

_____

_____

_____

_____

_____

_____

_____

_____

_____

_____

_____

_____

# FAST Goals

When thinking about the FAST skill, what would be three goals you have for improving your communication? Do you need to be more kind to yourself? Do you need to apologize less? Do you need to stick to your values more? Do you need to be more truthful? How will these goals improve your communication? How will they improve how you feel about yourself?

_____

_____

_____

_____

_____

_____

_____

_____

_____

_____

_____

_____

_____

_____

_____

_____

_____

_____

_____

_____

_____

_____

_____

_____

_____

# The Drama Triangle

The drama triangle, created by Dr. Stephen Karpman in the 1960s, is a depiction of dysfunctional exchanges or conflicts that we often engage in within interpersonal relationships. The drama triangle consists of three roles: the victim, the persecutor, and the rescuer. Within relationships and conflicts, these roles are interchangeable. The victim is someone who feels powerless, helpless, and ashamed. They often have poor problem-solving and decision-making skills, leading them to need to be rescued. The persecutor is often critical, controlling, and aggressive. They often enforce the rules through bullying and threats. Their role usually becomes obvious when they become resentful of rescuing or feel unappreciated. Rescuers feel as though their job is to soothe and comfort the victim. They participate in enabling behavior by reinforcing the victim's needs and taking attention away from their own needs. Their motivation is to avoid conflict.

Think about the people in your life who keep you stuck in the victim role. What do they do to keep you in the victim role? What does it feel like to be the victim? How do you know that you are being the victim? How can you overcome being the victim?

_____

_____

_____

_____

_____

_____

_____

_____

_____

_____

_____

_____

_____

_____

_____

_____

_____

_____

_____

_____

_____

# Acting as the Persecutor

Think about the people in your life who trigger you to assume the persecutor role. What do they do to make you feel like you need to become the persecutor? What does it feel like to be the persecutor? How do you know that you are being the persecutor? What behaviors do you display? How can you overcome being the persecutor?

_____

_____

_____

_____

_____

_____

_____

_____

_____

_____

_____

# The Drama Triangle
# in Everyday Life

Create a list of times in your life when you become the victim, the persecutor, or the rescuer. Think about what goes on for you physically, mentally, and emotionally when you take on each of those roles. Think about your environment, your mental state, and your physical state.

|  | VICTIM | PERSECUTOR | RESCUER |
|---|---|---|---|
| WHEN |  |  |  |
| WHERE |  |  |  |
| HOW |  |  |  |
| WHO |  |  |  |
| FEELINGS |  |  |  |
| PHYSICAL SENSATIONS |  |  |  |

# Validation of Others

People with BPD often have validation wounds or feel as though they aren't validated enough by others. This can leave us unsure about how to validate others in our lives. DBT can teach you to find and create validation for yourself and others.

**Pay attention:** Give the other person your full attention. Listen and observe mindfully and without judgment. Focus and make eye contact.

**Reflect to the person:** Repeat back what you observe to demonstrate that you understand and that you are paying attention. Have an open mind and do not take offense if you are wrong.

**Hidden messages:** Be aware of what's not being said. Pay attention to the other person's body language and what information you already know about the person.

**Understand:** Try to understand the other person from their point of view.

**Acknowledge the valid:** Acknowledge that you understand the other person's thoughts, beliefs, feelings, and actions given their current reality.

**Show equality:** Just be yourself. Treat the other person as an equal, not someone fragile or incapable.

Think of ways that you invalidate yourself and your feelings. How does it feel when you invalidate yourself? How can you improve your self-invalidation? Make a goal for improving your own self-invalidation by practicing three different types of self-validation every day. How might it feel to validate yourself regularly?

_____

_____

_____

_____

_____

_____

_____

_____

_____

_____

_____

_____

_____

# Validation of Others

Think about your interactions with others. How do you invalidate them without even thinking about it? How can you practice validating them more regularly? How might validating them improve your relationships?

_____

_____

_____

_____

_____

_____

_____

_____

_____

_____

_____

_____

_____

_____

_____

_____

_____

_____

_____

_____

_____

_____

_____

_____

_____

_____

_____

# Validation Scripts

Write out a validation script to practice for when you make
a mistake.

_____

_____

_____

_____

_____

_____

_____

Write out a validation script to practice for when you do
something great.

_____

_____

_____

_____

_____

_____

# Validation Scenarios

Practice validating others. Here are a few examples where a friend may need to feel validated. Write your validating statement in response to each example.

It's Tuesday night and your friend calls you crying. She tells you that her boyfriend of six months just broke up with her via text message.

_____

_____

_____

Your coworker, whom you typically eat lunch with, tells you that her cat died and she is feeling sad and lonely.

_____

_____

_____

On Wednesday morning, your younger brother calls to tell you that he has been accepted to a graduate school in California that he really wanted to attend.

_____

_____

_____

# Finding and Getting People to Like You

For many with BPD, relationships can be difficult to maintain due to fears of abandonment and struggles between intense admiration and devaluation, so it's important to know how to form healthy relationships. When looking for people to become friends with, a few key points can be helpful:

- Look for people who have similar interests as you, as it tends to be easier to keep friends that have similar attitudes, beliefs, and lifestyles.

- Make conversation: Ask questions about the other person and don't just talk about yourself. Don't interrupt; listen to listen, not just to respond.

- Express liking the other person equally. Find subtle things to compliment them on, but don't drown them in praise. It's a balance of showing and receiving interest from the other person. Remember to never use compliments as a way of obtaining a favor or something you want.

Thinking about a recent social situation, how could you join the conversation or group skillfully? What signified to you that this group was an open or closed group? How did this group show you that you would fit in with them? How can you prepare yourself for integrating into a group in the future?

_____

_____

_____

_____

_____

_____

_____

_____

_____

_____

_____

_____

_____

_____

_____

_____

_____

_____

_____

# Making New Friends

Reflecting on your daily activities, where is there an opportunity for you to create new friendships? What about these people signifies to you that you would enjoy being their friend? Do you have similar interests, hobbies, or beliefs? Think about forming a relationship with them. How can you approach them? What might the conversation look like? After approaching the person for the first time, how can you follow up and continue to foster the friendship?

_____

_____

_____

_____

_____

_____

_____

_____

_____

_____

_____

_____

# Friends in Common Places

Go to a place you enjoy visiting. While there, find a group of people you can imagine yourself being friends with and observe their conversation. Use the skills from the previous pages to join the group conversation.

What did you do?

_____

How did they react?

_____

How did the conversation go?

_____

How do you feel about the interaction?

_____

What would you change?

_____

What went well?

_____

# Ending Relationships

It can be difficult to know when to end a relationship. Relationships end for many reasons, but you have permission to leave any relationship that does not serve you, that hurts you, that is harmful for you, or that keeps you from reaching your goals. It is important to be in wise mind when ending a relationship, not emotion mind. If a relationship is important and not destructive or keeping you from meeting your goals, then using interpersonal skills to problem-solve can be effective. If you make the decision to end a relationship, use cope ahead to plan and manage ending the relationship. Remember to be direct and tell the other person exactly what you need; use DEAR MAN and GIVE FAST for communicating what you need.

*If you are in a life-threatening or abusive relationship, call a local domestic violence hotline or the National Domestic Violence Hotline at 1-800-799-7233.*

When have you stayed in a relationship that you needed to end? What about the relationship told you that you needed to end it? Did the relationship keep you from meeting your goals? Did the relationship threaten your physical or mental well-being? Did you find yourself putting in more work than the other person? Did you find yourself being invalidated?

---

---

---

---

---

# Pros and Cons of Ending Relationships

Practice pros and cons of ending a relationship that does not currently serve your needs.

|  | PROS | CONS |
|---|---|---|
| STAYING |  |  |
| LEAVING |  |  |

Write out a DEAR MAN for ending the relationship.

Describe:

_____

Express:

_____

Assert:

_____

Reinforce:

_____

(Stay) Mindful:

_____

Appear confident:

_____

Negotiate:

_____

_____

_____

_____

*I am worthy of love and kindness.*

# A Final Word

Congratulations on completing this DBT journey! My hope is that you found meaning, hope, and insight throughout your work during the time you spent navigating this journal. No matter where you are in your journey navigating the BPD experience with DBT, please continue exploring resources for success and improvement, as things will only continue to improve for you and your life!

# Resources

**Behavioral Tech**
BehavioralTech.org
Marsha Linehan's DBT training organization.

**National Education Alliance for Borderline Personality Disorder**
BorderlinePersonalityDisorder.org/links-to-other-bpd-sources
The NEABPD's webpage for resources and tools on living with
BPD.

**The Substance Abuse and Mental Health Services Administration**
SAMHSA.gov
The U.S. Department of Health and Human Services agency that
leads public health efforts to reduce the impact of substance
abuse and mental illness on America's communities.

*DBT Skills Training Manual* (2015) by Marsha Linehan
The training resource for DBT therapists who are teaching DBT
skills to clients.

# References

Berman, Robby. "New Study Suggests We Have 6,200 Thoughts Every Day." Big Think. July 16, 2020. BigThink.com /neuropsych/how-many-thoughts-per-day.

Johnson, R. Skip. "Escaping Conflict and the Karpman Drama Triangle." BPDFamily. January 3, 2020. BPDFamily.com /content/karpman-drama-triangle.

Linehan, Marsha M. *Cognitive-Behavioral Treatment of Borderline Personality Disorder*. New York: Guilford Press, 1993.

Linehan, Marsha M. *DBT Skills Training Manual*, 2nd ed. New York: Guilford Press, 2015.

"What Is Dialectical Behavior Therapy (DBT)?" BehaviorialTech .org. BehavioralTech.org/resources/faqs/dialectical-behavior -therapy-dbt.

# About the Author

 **Whitney Frost, LPC, C-DBT,** is a licensed professional counselor in Denver, Colorado, where she owns a private practice focusing on helping women navigate the struggles of BPD, bipolar disorder, infertility, and perinatal and postpartum mood disorders. Her practice focuses on providing quality mental health care to women in the greater Denver area regardless of their ability to pay. She is a mother of two and enjoys spending time with her family and volunteering in her free time.